W9-CSH-013

Homosexuality Around the World: Safe Havens, Cultural Challenges

The Gallup's Guide to Modern Gay, Lesbian, & Transgender Lifestyle

Homosexuality Around the World: Safe Havens, Cultural Challenges

by Jaime A. Seba

Mason Crest Publishers

Copyright © 2011 by Mason Crest Publishers. All rights reserved. No part of this publication may be reproduced or transmitted in any form or by any means, electronic or mechanical, including photocopying, recording, taping, or any information storage and retrieval system, without permission from the publisher.

MASON CREST PUBLISHERS INC.
370 Reed Road
Broomall, Pennsylvania 19008
(866)MCP-BOOK (toll free)
www.masoncrest.com

First Printing
9 8 7 6 5 4 3 2 1

Library of Congress Cataloging-in-Publication Data
Seba, Jaime.
  Homosexuality around the world : safe havens, cultural challenges / by Jaime Seba.
      p. cm. — (The Gallup's guide to modern gay, lesbian, & transgender lifestyle)
  Includes bibliographical references and index.
   ISBN 978-1-4222-1753-5   ISBN 978-1-4222-1758-0 (series)
   ISBN 978-1-4222-1872-3 (pbk.)   ISBN 978-1-4222-1863-1 (pbk series)
  1. Gays—Juvenile literature. 2. Gay rights—Juvenile literature. 3. Gays—Legal status, laws, etc.—Juvenile literature. I. Title.
   HQ76.26.S434 2011
   306.76'609051—dc22
                                    2010017917

Produced by Harding House Publishing Service, Inc.
www.hardinghousepages.com
Interior design by MK Bassett-Harvey.
Cover design by Torque Advertising + Design.
Printed in the USA by Bang Printing.

PICTURE CREDITS

Covarrubias, Alex; Creative Commons: p. 32
Creative Commons: pp. 15, 16, 38, 41, 44, 53
Folini, Franco; Creative Commons: p. 46
Giabbenelli, Philippe; Creative Commons: p. 27
Osado, Creative Commons: p. 28
Thelmadatter, Creative Commons: p. 30
Thomas, Dylan; Creative Commons: p. 19
Whitney, Lauren; Creative Commons: p. 57

Contents

Introduction

We are both individuals and community members. Our differences define individuality; our commonalities create a community. Some differences, like the ability to run swiftly or to speak confidently, can make an individual stand out in a way that is viewed as beneficial by a community, while the group may frown upon others. Some of those differences may be difficult to hide (like skin color or physical disability), while others can be hidden (like religious views or sexual orientation). Moreover, what some communities or cultures deem as desirable differences, like thinness, is a negative quality in other contemporary communities. This is certainly the case with sexual orientation and gender identity, as explained in *Homosexuality Around the World*, one of the volumes in this book series.

Often, there is a tension between the individual (individual rights) and the community (common good). This is easily visible in everyday matters like the right to own land versus the common good of building roads. These cases sometimes result in community controversy and often are adjudicated by the courts.

An even more basic right than property ownership, however, is one's gender and sexuality. Does the right of gender expression trump the concerns and fears of a community or a family or a school? *Feeling Wrong in Your Own Body*, as the author of that volume suggests, means confronting, in the most personal way, the tension between individuality and community. And, while a community, family, and school have the right (and obligation) to protect its children, does the notion of property rights extend to controlling young adults' choice as to how they express themselves in terms of gender or sexuality?

Changes in how a community (or a majority of the community) thinks about an individual right or responsibility often precedes changes in the law enacted by legislatures or decided by courts. And for these changes to occur, individuals (sometimes working in small groups) often defied popular opinion, political pressure, or religious beliefs. Some of these trends are discussed in *A New Generation of Homosexuality*. Every generation (including yours!) stands on the accomplishments of our ancestors and in *Gay and Lesbian Role Models* you'll be reading about some of them.

One of the most pernicious aspects of discrimination on the basis of sexual orientation is that "homosexuality" is a stigma that can be hidden (see the volume about *Homophobia*). While some of my generation (I was your age in the early 1960s) think that life is so much easier being "queer" in the age of the Internet, Gay-Straight Alliances, and Ellen, in reality, being different in areas where difference matters is *always* difficult. Coming Out, as described in the volume of the same title, is always challenging—for both those who choose to come out and for the friends and family they trust with what was once a hidden truth. Being healthy means being honest—at least to yourself. Having supportive friends and family is most important, as explained in *Being Gay, Staying Healthy.*

Sometimes we create our own "families"—persons bound together by love and identity but not by name or bloodline. This is quite common in gay communities today as it was several generations ago. Forming families or small communities based on rejection by the larger community can also be a double-edged sword. While these can be positive, they may also turn into prisons of conformity. Does being lesbian, for example, mean everyone has short hair, hates men, and drives (or rides on) a motorcycle? *What Does It Mean to Be Gay, Lesbian, Bisexual, or Transgender?* "smashes" these and other stereotypes.

Another common misconception is that "all gay people are alike"—a classic example of a stereotypical statement. We may be drawn together because of a common prejudice or oppression, but we should not forfeit our individuality for the sake of the safety of a common identity, which is one of the challenges shown in *Gay People of Color: Facing Prejudices, Forging Identities*.

Coming out to who *you* are is just as important as having a group or "family" within which to safely come out. Becoming knowledgeable about these issues (through the books in this series and the other resources to which they will lead), feeling good about yourself, behaving safely, actively listening to others *and* to your inner spirit—all this will allow you to fulfill your promise and potential.

James T. Sears, PhD
Consultant

chapter 1

A Global Community

Imagine seven friends sitting in a room, chatting. They talk about the latest Hollywood blockbusters. They trade stories about their lives and families. They laugh at shared memories. They complain about their jobs. They discuss vacation plans.

They are all about the same age. They are all gay men. They have all had committed, long-term relationships.

But the world sees each of them differently.

Mark is from Australia, where his hometown hosts one of the largest gay and lesbian pride festivals in the world.

Prasad is from India, where up until 2009, he could have been put in prison for being gay.

Tim is from Great Britain, which has rapidly been expanding legal protections to gay people since the beginning of the new millennium, including allowing gay couples to adopt and form civil unions.

Clint is from South Africa, where, despite decades of intolerance under Apartheid, gay marriage is now legal.

It's also legal in Canada, where Robin lives.

Jasper is from Holland, which has historically been one of the world's most **progressive** cultures and where now gay couples have all the same rights as straight couples.

Eric is from the United States, where the federal government does not recognize same-sex marriages; gay people can be fired from their jobs and in some states, homosexual behavior was illegal until 2003.

What's That Mean?

Progressive ideas are those that support social change in support of human freedom and progress.

The rights of a citizen to personal and political freedom under the law are known as **civil rights**.

"It's very surprising to me that so many other countries around the globe are so far ahead of us when it comes to basic **civil rights**, like marriage," says Eric. "We always think of America as being a leader in the world, but when it comes to this, we're pretty far behind."

As a professional in the travel industry, Eric has traveled all over the world, visiting five of the seven continents. And he's had the opportunity to experience how other countries treat their gay and lesbian citizens. Having grown up in a Catholic family, attending a Catholic school, he is always surprised and interested to see the ways

EXTRA INFO

Apartheid (which means "separateness" in Afrikaans) was a system of legal racial segregation enforced by the government in South Africa between 1948 and 1994, under which the rights of the majority non-white inhabitants of South Africa were curtailed and minority rule by white people was maintained. After 1958, black people were deprived of citizenship in their country, legally becoming citizens instead of one of ten tribally based self-governing homelands called Bantustans, four of which became nominally independent states. The government segregated education, medical care, and other public services, and provided black people with services inferior to those of white people.

Apartheid was not friendly to gays. During the 1970s and '80s in South Africa, army psychiatrists aided by chaplains ferreted out suspected homosexuals from the armed forces, sending them to military psychiatric units. Those who could not be "cured" with drugs, aversion shock therapy, hormone treatment, and other radical "psychiatric" means were chemically castrated or given sex-change operations. Although the exact number is not known, former Apartheid army surgeons estimate that as many as 900 forced "sexual reassignment" operations may have been performed between 1971 and 1989 at military hospitals, as part of a top-secret program to root out homosexuality from the service.

other people around the world have **integrated** religion with gay and lesbian issues.

"So much of American culture is impacted by religion, especially in certain regions," he notes. "But other parts of the world aren't like that. Even in Spain, which is so heavily influenced by the Roman Catholic Church, they allow same-sex marriage and are very accepting of gay people. They are able to keep the two things separate. I don't understand why we can't do that here (in America)."

What's That Mean?

Integrated means fitting together in a way that makes sense.

More than a decade before Vermont became the first American state to offer civil unions to homosexual couples; Europe was already leading the way. In 1989, Denmark broke new ground as it became the first country to provide legislation protecting same-sex couples. Though church weddings were not allowed, Danish law granted gay couples the same rights as heterosexual married couples.

By 1996, Norway, Sweden, and Iceland each had similar laws, with Finland following six years later. The Netherlands enacted laws allowing for full civil marriage rights for gay couples in 2001, and two years later its neighbor to the south, Belgium, did the same.

That trend of tolerance continued throughout Western Europe in the new millennium. Germany, which borders Belgium and the Netherlands, protects gay couples with regard to inheritance and tenants' rights, and it has provided a same-sex couples' register (granting them certain legal rights) since 2001. Neighboring France also has limited protections for

EXTRA INFO

When U.S. politicians say they support civil unions but not marriage for people of the same sex, what do they mean?

There are three main differences between civil unions and marriage:

1. The right to federal benefits from the U.S. government. States that allow some type of same-sex union are able to grant only state rights. The Defense of Marriage Act passed in 1996 prohibits same-sex couples from receiving federal marriage rights and benefits.
2. Because civil unions are not recognized by all states, such agreements are not always valid when couples cross state lines.
3. "Marriage" is a term that carries with it religious and cultural meaning. That's important to both sides of the controversy, both gay rights activists and those who don't believe gays should marry.

same-sex couples, though they do not include full marriage rights.

By 2005, Luxembourg and Britain also permitted their own versions of same-sex civil union laws and protections, and Spain had legalized gay marriage and adoption.

Similarly, a Canadian bill to legalize same-sex marriage became law in 2005, though it was already legal in eight of the country's ten provinces. And despite significant **homophobia** throughout Africa, a South African high court ruled in 2005 that it was unconstitutional to deny same-sex couples the right to marry, and that country's laws were **amended** within a year.

What's That Mean?

Homophobia is the fear and hatred of gay and lesbian people.

Something that has been **amended** has been officially modified, or changed.

Argentina became the first Latin American country to allow same-sex civil unions in 2003. The following year Australia's first civil unions were allowed in Tasmania. Much like the United States, individual states and territories in Australia decide whether civil unions are permitted. The difference, though, is that the federal government then recognizes those partnerships.

Overall attitudes toward homosexuality in Australia are also very similar to the United States. Depending

Gay Pride parades take place around the world. This one was in Tel Aviv, Israel

on the region of the country, public opinion and perception can vary widely. "Australia is accepting, in that you don't fear for your life or anything like that, the way maybe you do in some other countries," states Mark, who works for an airline and has visited countries all over the world. "But there are still people who are very rigid in their belief that being gay is wrong, and they're not afraid to share those feelings. On the whole, though, the younger generation is much more tolerant, which I think is the case in the States and similar cultures."

Sydney's Gay and Lesbian Mardi Gras festival is an elaborate event. Here, Tina Arena and Alison Jiear perform "No More Tears (Enough Is Enough)."

Sydney, the largest city in Australia, is host to the annual Gay and Lesbian Mardi Gras festival, one of the world's most famous pride celebrations held in support of the gay and lesbian community. And Australia is one of the twenty-four countries worldwide that allows gay and lesbian people to serve openly in the military.

In 2010, American President Barack Obama announced his desire to end the "Don't Ask, Don't Tell" law that prohibits openly gay and lesbian soldiers from serving in the military. At that time, the United States was one of only six NATO member countries that did not allow gay people to serve openly in the armed forces. The countries that did allow it included Austria, Belgium, Canada, the Czech Republic, Denmark, Estonia, Finland, France, Germany, Ireland, Israel, Italy, Lithuania, Luxembourg, the Netherlands, New Zealand, Norway, Slovenia, South Africa, Spain, Sweden, Switzerland and the United Kingdom, according to the Center for the Study of Sexual Minorities in the Military.

Until the end of the twentieth century, the United Kingdom had largely mirrored the United States in terms of gay rights. The infamous 1969 police raid on a gay bar, the Stonewall Inn, in New York sparked riots against intolerance toward the gay community by police and government in America. It also prompted England's own gay rights movements. But over the next three decades, just as equal protections under the law came slowly in the United States, Britain appeared slow to recognize its gay citizens, that is until the end of the twentieth century.

The first decade of the new millennium saw the overturning of a law that prohibited teaching gay history in British schools, gay couples legally permitted to adopt children, and legally recognized civil unions. Perhaps more importantly, a 2009 survey showed that 61 percent of British respondents felt gay couples should be allowed to legally marry, and 51 percent felt children in schools should be taught that gay unions are equal to straight marriage.

"That was the most pleasant surprise from this poll. In this matter it is parents who are the ones who matter and clearly they are much more realistic about the wider world than veteran opponents of equality," says Ben Summerskill, who runs a charity supporting the gay community in the UK.

Tim spent much of that decade traveling abroad, so when he returned home, he was delighted to see that laws in England had reached and exceeded the standards set by other countries around the world. "Unions, adoption, more acceptance by the church, equal rights—it's like a whole new England!" says Tim. "The gay community has been waiting a long time for this, and I think now the rest of the country was getting impatient, too. And I think we're going to see this happening in other parts of the world, too. We already do."

Perhaps the most gay-friendly place on earth is Holland. Long known as a haven for gay people because of its progressive policies, it was the first country in the world to legalize same-sex marriage. Jasper says it's difficult to think about the history of gay rights in his country because they have just always been there.

In Amsterdam, the Gay Pride Parade takes place on the canals.

"I was born in the Netherlands where homosexuality was legalized in 1911," he says. "During the Second World War, it was made illegal again by the Nazis, but in 1945, the law was reinstated. Gay marriage was legalized in 2001. Of course, you always will have people who are strongly against gay people due to their religion or their personal opinion. But the Netherlands is, in my opinion, one of the most progressive and open countries in the world when it comes to gay rights, being gay, and same-sex marriages."

Jasper and his partner of more than ten years now live on the Caribbean island of Curacao, a territory of the Kingdom of the Netherlands. "Although homosexuality is accepted on the islands, it is not as free and open as in the mainland," he says. "It is quite funny but most locals seem to be very open about the topic as long as it does not 'run in their family.' I've been living in Curacao for the last fifteen years and have not encountered any hate or anger towards me because of my sexual orientation."

As a whole, the Caribbean region is still noted as being one of the world's most intolerant areas toward gay and lesbian people, particularly in Jamaica. But the tide is changing. In Cuba, the influence of President Raul Castro's daughter Mariela, a strong supporter of gay rights, has led to increased tolerance and acceptance. Jasper has seen his small island becoming increasingly accepting, recognizing marriages conducted in Holland and hosting pride festivals that attract visitors from neighboring islands. And like Curacao, other islands such as Puerto Rico, the Cayman Islands, and the Turks and Caicos Islands have done away with laws prohibiting homosexual behavior. This is largely due to the strong influence of the European nations on which the islands are dependant.

In 2008, the United Nations issued its first-ever statement condemning human rights violations based on sexual orientation or gender identity. The statement was issued by the U.N. General Assembly on behalf of sixty-six member states: Albania, Andorra, Argentina, Armenia, Australia, Austria, Belgium, Bolivia, Bosnia and Herzegovina, Brazil, Bulgaria, Canada, Cape Verde, Central African Republic, Chile, Colombia, Croatia, Cuba, Cyprus, Czech Republic, Denmark, Ecuador, Estonia, Finland, France, Gabon, Georgia, Germany, Greece, Guinea-Bissau, Hungary, Iceland, Ireland, Israel, Italy, Japan, Latvia, Liechtenstein, Lithuania, Luxembourg, Malta, Mauritius, Mexico, Montenegro, Nepal, Netherlands, New Zealand, Nicaragua, Norway, Paraguay, Poland, Portugal, Romania, San Marino, Sao Tome and Principe, Serbia, Slovakia, Slovenia, Spain, Sweden, Switzerland, the former Yugoslav Republic of Macedonia, Timor-Leste, United Kingdom, Uruguay, and

Venezuela. The issue had been **polarizing** in the U.N., as many Muslim nations refused to sign because of their opposition to homosexuality. The United States was also not among the document's supporters until March 2009, when newly sworn-in American President Barack Obama's administration signed on.

What's That Mean?

An issue that is *polarizing* is strongly divides public opinion, either for or against.

"The United States is an outspoken defender of human rights and critic of human rights abuses around the world," State Department spokesman Robert Wood said. "As such, we join with the other supporters of this Statement and we will continue to remind countries of the importance of respecting the human rights of all people."

FIND OUT MORE ON THE INTERNET

International Gay and Lesbian Human Rights Commission
www.iglhrc.org

LGBT Legal Status Around the World (Amnesty International USA)
www.amnestyusa.org/lgbt-human-rights/country-information/page.do?id = 1106576

READ MORE ABOUT IT

Maran, Meredith. *50 Ways to Support Lesbian and Gay Equality*. San Francisco, Calif.: New World Library, 2005.

Newton, David E. *Gay and Lesbian Rights: A Reference Handbook*. Santa Barbara, Calif.: ABC-CLIO, 2009.

chapter 2

America's Neighbors

When the popular American gay television series *Queer as Folk* wrapped up its fifth and final season, fans wondered what would become of the beloved collection of characters from Pittsburgh, Pennsylvania. The question was especially important for characters Lindsay and Melanie, the lesbian parents of two young children. As a proposed law to limit legal rights of gay parents loomed on the horizon, and a horrific hate crime shook their quiet community, they questioned whether their family could find safety and security in the United States.

"The ones who [hate us] no longer have to do it behind our backs," Melanie said. "They can do it in the White House, in the churches, on television, in the streets! Is that the kind of place we want to live? Is that the kind of place we want to raise our kids?"

The show's fictitious Proposition 14, which sought to bar gay and lesbian people from a variety of civil and parental rights, depicted the same threats that confronted gay and lesbian people in real-life across the United States in 2005, when the final episode aired. The intolerant attitudes shown in Pittsburgh reflected the sweeping tide of homophobia throughout the country that coincided with the re-election of President George W. Bush in 2004, when eleven states also approved constitutional amendments banning gay marriage.

Melanie and Lindsay's ultimate solution was to pack up and head north, relocating their family to Canada.

Though some fans argued that the couple should have stayed and continued the battle for ***domestic*** equality, the move was not an unusual notion. In the days following the 2004 election, traffic on the website for Citizenship and Immigration in Canada hit an all-time high. That's because while American political trends were reducing the rights of gay and lesbian citizens, Canada's House of Commons voted to guarantee full marriage rights to same-sex couples in 2005. The move made Canada the world's third country to recognize gay marriage, after Holland and Belgium.

"The big peaceable kingdom on the U.S. border will demonstrate that it is absolutely possible for

What's That Mean?

Domestic has to do with people's living arrangements and family life.

EXTRA INFO

Hate crimes are violent acts against victims who are targeted because of their race, religion, gender, sexual orientation or other minority status. Gay and lesbian people have long been the victims of both organized and random hate crimes, but because of their fear of exposure as gay people, and because of many law enforcement agencies' lack of interest in prosecuting these crimes, the vast majority of hate crimes have gone unreported. The FBI officially reported just over 1000 hate crimes against gay and lesbian people in the U.S. in 2009, but the number is no doubt much higher. The brutal hate-crime murder of University of Wyoming freshman Matthew Shepard in 1998 brought the issue to the American public and on October 28, 2009 President Obama signed the Matthew Shepard Hate Crimes Prevention Act, into law. The Act expands the 1969 United States federal hate-crime law (which protected victims of hate crimes based on race or religion) to include crimes motivated by a victim's actual or perceived gender, sexual orientation, gender identity, or disability. The Act gives federal authorities, like the FBI, greater authority to investigate homophobia-motivated hate crimes and provides funding for state and local law enforcement to pursue and prosecute those who commit these crimes. The Act is the first federal law to extend legal protections to LGBT victims of hate crimes and was supported by thirty-one state Attorneys General and over 210 national law enforcement, professional, education, civil rights, religious, and civic organizations.

religious freedom to coexist with the end of discrimination against gay and lesbian people," Alex Munter, a Canadian gay rights advocate, told *The Washington Post* on the day of the vote. "Many couples already come from America to get married, and now thousands more will come."

Prior to the national vote, gay marriage had already been recognized in some provinces across Canada, and Americans were already taking advantage of the opportunity. On June 1, 2005, Alex Ali and Lynn Warren were married in Ottawa. The American gay

Participants in a Gay Pride parade in Vancouver, Canada, focus on bringing rights to members of the GLBT community who live in nations that are not as tolerant as Canada.

couple had gained international attention as competitors on the reality television show *The Amazing Race*. But when they were unable to get married in their home state of California, Ottawa radio station Hot 89.9 invited them north of the border to get married in Canada.

The couple expected to see protestors, as was common in the United States. They didn't. Instead, they saw only fans and other friendly faces. The experience was so positive that they encouraged other couples to come and see for themselves.

"It's a big world. Come to Canada, come to Ottawa and have a beautiful wedding and celebrate your love. And be with people who celebrate instead of tolerate," Warren said.

Canadians are proud of their nation's progressive stance on same-sex marriage.

Canadian law does not have a residency requirement when it comes to marriage, meaning that couples from anywhere in the world can come to Canada to have their marriage legally performed. Whether it's recognized in their home country, though, is another matter. In the United States, the Defense of Marriage Act, signed into law by President Bill Clinton in 1996, limits the recognition of marriage to being between one man and one woman only, regardless of whether same-sex marriages are recognized by other countries.

What's That Mean?

Disparity means a major, unequal difference.

The historic Canadian ruling led many to note the *disparity* between Canada and the United States when it comes to gay rights and freedom. America was no longer at the forefront of equality and justice even within North America, as Mexico has also made strong statements in support of its gay and lesbian citizens.

In March 2010, Mexico City became the first Latin American region to legalize same-sex marriage. Similar laws in other areas of the country followed this progressive turn. But despite such advances, public opinion in the diverse nation is not changing as quickly. Mexico's population is divided among wealthier metropolitan areas that thrive on tourism and poorer rural communities where cultural

Drag queens dressed in traditional Mexican clothing participate in a Gay Pride parade in Mexico City. However, smaller Mexican communities are far less tolerant of such open displays of homosexuals.

tradition and religion often dictate social trends. Those traditions, which are highly influenced by the **conservative** Catholic Church, make it difficult for gay men and women to live their lives openly, particularly outside the major cities in Mexico.

Irving Cabanas lives in Playa del Carmen, a coastal tourist destination. Though he says his hometown is a very welcoming place, he knows there's a limit to what his neighbors and even his family will accept.

What's That Mean?

Conservative means resistant to social change and new ideas.

"I [travel] around the world, and I have found many different ways people [react] toward gays. There are so many cities that do not care what people do with their lives, and they do respect us," said Irving Cabanas, who travels internationally for business. "In Mexico, they prefer to see someone married [to a woman] even though he is more gay than straight. It is very sad, because people pretend to be something they are not in order to keep their families and friends, which does not make sense [because] family and friends should always have their arms open if they really love you, no matter what!"

Irving's family and a few friends know he is gay, but it is rarely acknowledged in conversations. Though this prevents him from sharing some of the most important events in his life, including the painful ending of a long-term relationship, Irving recognizes that these things can't be rushed.

"[It] is my private life and is hard sometimes to belong to a circle when you are different," he said. "I do my business and no one knows. My sisters know, but we never talk about it. I never go out with them to gay clubs or talk about guys and things like that. With my friends [it] is the same, and the reason I do that is because I am scared that people take it the wrong way. One day a friend of mine said, 'I don't mind gay people at all.' But I asked her if she had a

The Mexican territory shown as light blue in this map is covered by a constitutional anti-discrimination law that prohibits discrimination based on sexual orientation. As of 2007, the Mexican state of Coahuila and the capital Mexico City (dark blue) have approved civil unions that also apply for same-sex couples.

gay son, will she accept it, and she answered very angry, 'My son will never be gay.'"

But while he fears losing the respect and love of his friends, Irving is not concerned about violence. He has never experienced or witnessed any such acts because of homophobia, and he has rarely heard of them on television. But he recognizes that his home city, because it is larger and more developed, is not representative of all of Mexico. The key, he said, is education and understanding.

As that education grows and worldwide acceptance of gay rights and inclusion increases, Irving recognizes that he may not always feel the need to keep his personal life so private. He hopes that Mexico will follow in the footsteps of Canada, Holland, and other countries around the world in being more tolerant of gay people. And if there comes a time where he needs to take a stand for himself and his community in Mexico, he's prepared to do that.

"If one day I feel that I have to put this into a balance, I would not be afraid to show who I am," he said.

FIND OUT MORE ON THE INTERNET

Egale Canada (National Gay Rights Organization
www.egale.ca/

LGBT Rights in Mexico
en.wikipedia.org/wiki/LGBT_rights_in_Mexico

READ MORE ABOUT IT

Guttmann, Matthew C. *The Meanings of Macho: Being a Man in Mexico City.* Berkeley, Calif.: University of California Press, 1996.

Rayside, David M. *Queer Inclusions, Continental Division: Public Recognition of Sexual Diversity in Canada and the United States.* Toronto, Can.: University of Toronto Press, 2008.

chapter 3

Oppression Overseas

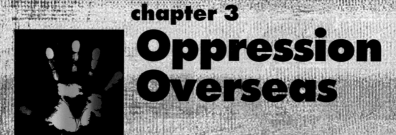

When vacationers think of Jamaica, some classic Caribbean images come to mind: the bright beaming sun, clear blue waters, stretches of sandy beaches. It seems like the perfect destination.

But when it comes to being gay in Jamaica, the picture is significantly different: mob violence, public attacks, hate speech, and extreme homophobia.

"Jamaica is the worst any of us has ever seen," Rebecca Schleifer of the U.S.-based Human Rights Watch told *Time Magazine*.

In 2006, *Time* profiled the place that human rights groups referred to as the most homophobic place on earth. It was a glimpse into the dark world were extreme violence against homosexuals is supported by the community and even the government. The country's two most well-known gay rights activists were murdered, and a crowd celebrated over one of the mutilated bodies. When a father discovered his teenage son was gay, he encouraged a mob to lynch the boy. Police reportedly cheered on a group that stabbed and stoned a gay man to death.

The following year, residents in an East Kingston community gave notice that their gay neighbors had two weeks to leave, according to *The Jamaica Star*. At the end, on what was referred to as Gay Eradication Day, community members vowed to use any means necessary to eliminate gay people from their neighborhood. The gay people reportedly fled by the end of the warning period.

What's That Mean?

Something that's *taboo* is forbidden by society.

"There were continuing reports of mob violence against people, mostly men, perceived to be involved in same-sex relationships," stated Amnesty International's 2009 report on human rights in Jamaica. "The true extent of attacks on gay men was unknown as the subject is *taboo* and people do not report attacks for fear of exposure."

That fear also affects community groups traditionally associated with the gay community in other countries. Unlike the major HIV and AIDS organizations more familiar to Americans, Jamaica AIDS Support for Life makes a point of distancing itself from the gay community. The organization's website clearly features images of heterosexual couples and families and contains no mention of the gay community.

Four of Jamaica's top dancehall music stars were mocked and ridiculed as "Killer Queens" in a Gay Pride parade in London, UK, which was dedicated to the memory of murdered Jamaican gay rights campaigner, Brian Williamson. The Mayor of London, Ken Livingstone, formally endorsed the protest against Jamaica, saying that he condemned "homophobic lyrics that incite violence against lesbians and gays."

What's That Mean?

Something that is *rampant* is powerful and uncontrolled.

Evangelical Christianity is a form of Protestant Christianity that began in the 1700s. Evangelicals believe in the need for personal conversion (what they call being "born again"); they believe that most of the Bible's directions are to be taken literally; and they emphasize the importance of the death and resurrection of Jesus. In the twentieth and twenty-first centuries, American evangelicals have become increasingly political, taking an actively conservative stance.

In April of 2010, JASL held its first tolerance walk in support of people living with HIV and AIDS. Numerous community groups participated, including gay and lesbian organizations. Though international media treated this as a step forward for gay equality, the coverage in Jamaica was quite different. A headline in the *Jamaican Observer* screamed "It Wasn't a Gay March!" and JASL workers quickly separated their organization from anything related to gay issues.

The reason for this isn't hard to imagine. Considering the severe and rampant homophobia in the country, JASL organizers were concerned that people in need would not seek testing or treatment because of a fear of being labeled as gay. "They think they are going to a gay organization, people don't want to come no more," Sharlene Kessna Duncans told the *Observer*. "They think that Jamaica AIDS Support is not just HIV, it is a gay thing, but JASL is for everyone."

Many attribute this ***rampant*** hatred to the influence of homophobic reggae music on popular culture. Jamaican musician Buju Banton became notorious among international gay activists in 1992 with the release of his song "Boom Bye-Bye", in which he says that gay people "haffi dead" ("have to die") and he brags about shooting them with Uzis and burning their skin with acid "like an old tire wheel." Banton was accused of being involved in a 2004 incident when a group of men broke into a house and brutally beat several gay men, but the case was dismissed due to a lack of evidence.

Those violent sentiments are not limited to Jamaica in the Caribbean. Singer Lieutenant, who hails from the tiny island of Martinique, once told his fans, "I kill the fags." In neighboring Guadeloupe, singer Admiral T's lyrics include encouraging people to burn gay people like cigarettes. And homosexuality is a crime in Barbados, also a popular tourist destination.

Many of these attitudes are deeply imbedded in traditional cultures and religion, often because homosexuality is considered a threat to the family. These beliefs are also commonly held in Africa, which is largely influenced by its Christian-based religion and family-oriented cultures.

In 2009, thousands of people welcomed three American ***evangelical*** Christians to Uganda. The visitors, invited by the Ugandan Parliament, came to give a series of lectures on topics including "The Gay

Movement's Agenda for Control of Society" and "The Gay Movement's Blueprints for Transforming a Nation."

Scott Lively, a Massachusetts pastor and attorney, was one of the three speakers. He spoke to audiences about the danger gay people have posed to families

EXTRA INFO

Many Evangelical churches are actively against all forms of homosexuality, believing that homosexuality is both a choice and a sin, but most of these groups would teach that it is wrong to treat a gay person unkindly. They would say, however, that homosexuals need to be saved from their sin. This perspective is expressed well by theologian Lehman Strauss:

> We must always keep before us the fact that homosexuals, like all of us sinners, are the objects of God's love. The Bible says, "But God commendeth His love toward us, in that while we were yet sinners, Christ died for us" (Romans 5:8). . . . The Christian who shares God's love for lost sinners will seek to reach the homosexual with the gospel of Christ, which "is the power of God unto salvation, to every one that believeth" (Romans 1:16). As a Christian I should hate all sin but I can find no justification for hating the sinner. The homosexual is a precious soul for whom Christ died. We Christians can show him the best way of life by pointing him to Christ.

Conservative Evangelicals spoke out against political and humanitarian action that could be seen as encouraging homosexuality in Africa. This position is controversial, as demonstrated by the protesters standing behind the Evangelical speaker here.

and children, sharing stories about **pedophiles** and child abusers. He addressed the need to effectively deal with "the homosexual issue" for the sake of a strong community.

The lecture series also included the topic "Effective Response to the Gay Agenda." "If somebody comes charging through the door with a machete and says, 'I'm going to attack this woman here with the machete,' am I going to tolerate that person coming to do that? No. I'm going to have zero tolerance for that," Lively told the crowd. "If your definition of homosexuality is being able to do whatever you want to and that you should be able to go and engage in sex with another person, and because of that, the disease you have is going to spread to that person, and they're going to take it home and give it to their wife, how much tolerance should we have for that? We should have zero tolerance for that."

The following month, Uganda apparently came up with its "effective response" when the Anti-Homosexuality Bill of 2009 was introduced in Parliament. The bill would impose a death sentence for homosexual behavior.

What's That Mean?

Pedophiles are people who sexually abuse children; the great majority of pedophiles are *not* homosexuals.

"What these people have done is set the fire they can't quench," Ugandan Reverend Kapya Kaoma, who attended the conference, said of three American visitors. "(They) underestimated the homophobia in Uganda (and) what it means to Africans when you speak about a certain group trying to destroy their children and their families. . . . When you speak like that, Africans will fight to the death."

The proposed bill prompted outrage around the world. Even the United States, which had previously supplied millions of dollars in aid in Uganda under President George W. Bush for teaching **abstinence,** now joined several other countries in threatening to withhold foreign aid. Faced with this possibility, the Ugandan government conceded to consider reducing the penalty for homosexuality to life in prison.

There was also uproar in American over the affect the three speakers had on this **controversial** law. Lively said he met privately with Ugandan leaders as an advisor, and the other speakers stated that the bill was not the intended result of their conference.

"I'm really no different than someone that's invited to Capitol Hill to give testimony before the

What's That Mean?

Abstinence means not having sex at all.

Something that is *controversial* creates strong feelings on both sides of an issue.

American legislature decides on what they're going to do in law," Lively said of his part in the creation of the Ugandan bill. "I don't have any special power to influence these people. They asked for my opinion, and I gave it."

Elsewhere in Africa, where being homosexual is still illegal in numerous countries, gay people have been victims of homophobic violence from police, hospitals, businesses, employers, and the government.

This is especially significant in terms of HIV and AIDS, which is a massive health crisis in Africa where more than 25 million people are living with the disease. The International Gay and Lesbian Human Rights Commission released a report in 2007 documenting examples of how gay men and women were denied medical treatment because of their sexual orientation. This included the story of a twenty-three-year-old gay man in Kenya who was chased out of a public health clinic when he sought treatment for a sexually transmitted disease. The report demonstrated how homophobic attitudes contributed to the African AIDS epidemic.

What's That Mean?

Consensual means that the two people involved in an activity are both doing so of their own free will.

To **flout** something is to very publically ignore it as a way of making a point.

Uganda's proposal to execute people for being gay is not unique in the world. In Iran, the government publicly hanged two men for homosexual behavior in 2005. "The execution of two men for **consensual** sexual activity is an outrage," said Jessica Stern, researcher with the Lesbian, Gay, Bisexual and Transgender Rights Program at Human Rights Watch. "The Iranian government's persecution of gay men *flouts* international human rights standards."

In much of the Middle East, homosexuality is forbidden under religious laws, which led to the arrest of fifty-two gay men in Egypt in 2001.

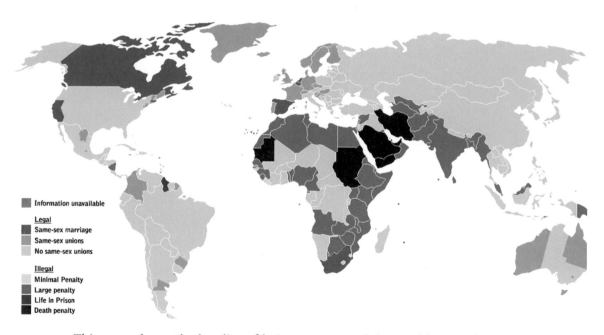

Information unavailable

Legal
Same-sex marriage
Same-sex unions
No same-sex unions

Illegal
Minimal Penalty
Large penalty
Life in Prison
Death penalty

This map shows the legality of being gay around the world. Note that some of the countries of Africa and the Middle East imposed the most severe penalties.

American Muslims tend to be more liberal than their Middle Eastern counterparts. In San Francisco, some Muslims even take part in the annual Gay Pride parade.

In 2008, a gay and lesbian rights demonstration in Russia was marred by physical assaults and arrests.

Such occurrences on the global stage have led human rights groups such as Amnesty International and the United Nations Commission on Human Rights to encourage other nations to take a stand.

"When a person deviates from what is considered 'normal' behavior they are targeted for violence. This is

EXTRA INFO

In many countries in the Middle East, homosexuality is punishable by shari'a, Islamic law. In some Muslim countries, the punishment is a death sentence. However, same-sex activities in private are considered to be commonplace in many Muslim nations. This is usually accepted, so long as a "homosexual" lifestyle is not openly adopted. Many conservative Muslims see the label of "homosexuality" as a sign of Western culture and its influence on Islamic ways of life. These people would argue that there was no label before the West got involved—people did what they wanted to in private, but they would eventually become part of a heterosexual marriage, and no one felt the need to proclaim themselves as "gay." Same-gender marriage would not even be a consideration for most Muslims. Instead, they believe that because the purpose of a marriage is to produce children, a true marriage can only exist between a man and a woman.

particularly acute when combined with discrimination on the basis of sexual orientation or change of gender identity," said Radhika Coomaraswamy, UN Special Rapporteur to the Fifty-Eighth Session of the Commission on Human Rights in 2002. "Violence against sexual minorities is on the increase and it is important that we take up the challenge of what may be called the last frontier of human rights."

The United Nations includes sexual orientation and gender identity in the protection outlined by the Commission on Human Rights.

FIND OUT MORE ON THE INTERNET

Gay Jamaica: Crime and Punishment
www.globalgayz.com/country/Jamaica/view/JAM/gay-jamaica-crime-and-punishment

Homosexuality is Not Un-African
gayrights.change.org/blog/view/homosexuality_is_not_un-african

READ MORE ABOUT IT

Epprecht, Marc. *Heterosexual Africa? The History of an Idea from the Age of Exploration to the Age of AIDS.* Athens, Ohio: Ohio University Press, 2008.

Luongo, Michael T. *Gay Travels in the Muslim World.* New York: Routledge, 2007.

chapter 4

Moving Ahead

Despite significant anti-gay attitudes and laws in African countries such as Zimbabwe and Nigeria, where being gay is illegal, there are signs of hope on the continent.

When Nelson Mandela was sworn in as president of South Africa in 1994, it signaled the end of the period of intolerance and oppression under the Apartheid government. At that time, South Africa became one of the world's first nations that outlawed discrimination based on sexual orientation, and by 1998, laws *criminalizing* homosexual behavior had been overturned. The move was reflective of the South African government's goal of eliminating all forms of discrimination in the country.

"The court has said that lesbians and gay men . . . have a right to equality and dignity and privacy," said Zackie Ach-

What's That Mean?

Criminalizing means making something illegal and subject to prosecution.

mat, director of South Africa's National Coalition for Gay and Lesbian Equality.

Prior to the end of Apartheid, homosexuality was punishable by up to seven years in prison. In fact, men weren't even permitted to have contact socially that could be considered gay behavior. Now even the military protects the rights of gay and lesbian soldiers.

"We are bound to fulfill the promises of democracy which we made to the people of our country," said South African Defense Minister Mosiuoa Lekota. "Are we going to suppress this so-called minority, or are we going to let these people enjoy the privilege of choosing who will be their life partners?"

Lekota's statements were made as part of a passionate plea to Parliament in 2006. The previous year, South Africa's high court had ruled that language in the country's law defining marriage as being between a man and a woman conflicted with the country's constitution, which prohibits discrimination based on sexual orientation.

The resulting Civil Union Bill was then presented to Parliament in November 2006. When Lekota spoke in favor of the bill, he encouraged his listeners to remember that the country had relied on the support of all of its citizens during the nation's fight for freedom from Apartheid, including gay and lesbian people.

"In the long and arduous struggle for democracy, very many men and women of homosexual or lesbian orientation joined the ranks of the liberation and democratic forces," Lekota told Parliament. "How then can we live with the reality that we should enjoy rights that together we fought for side by side, and deny them that?

Today, as we reap the fruits of democracy, it is only right that they must be afforded similar space in the sunshine of our democracy. . . . This country cannot afford to continue to be a prisoner of the backward, timeworn prejudices that have no basis."

Parliament agreed, and the bill passed by a vote of 230 to 41, making South Africa the fifth country in the world to legalize gay marriage.

This progressive attitude made Clint proud to live in a country that is a role model to other nations. He lives openly gay in Cape Town, the country's legislative capital, and he sees much more tolerance towards gay and lesbian people. But he knows there is still work to be done.

"We're always cautious because you never know if that law will change," said Clint. "Many people are not happy about it in South Africa."

Specifically, the Roman Catholic Church and some Muslim groups have spoken out to protest the law, and Parliamentary representatives from the African

Christian Democratic Party voted against the bill. Instances of homophobia-related crimes also still occur, especially in smaller cities and towns.

"[The response] forced us to confront the deep-seated prejudice and intolerance against gays and lesbians," said Melanie Judge, a program manager for the South African gay rights group OUT. "It's a day-to-day reality. . . . It's been quite a frightening process to see the level of hatred that has been openly expressed against this minority."

But for now, Clint is optimistic that the longer the country continues with equal rights, the more commonplace it will become, both at home and abroad.

During World War II, gays in Germany were rounded up with Jews and gypsies, and put into concentration camps. Today, however, open displays of affection between gay couples in Germany, like that shown here, are everyday sights.

"Change takes time, but the movement has been very positive," he said. "So I'm hopeful."

Similarly, progress in gay and lesbian rights is moving forward rapidly in India. It wasn't until 2009 that India decriminalized homosexuality. Prior to that point, it had been punishable by up to ten years in prison in a law introduced when India was under British rule. But the ruling by the Delhi High Court indicated a trend that gay and lesbian people in India had already seen coming.

"Since the early 1990s gay culture existed in the shadows and emerged at monthly parties and bar nights in a few cities, movie screenings, and counseling groups," said Keith D'Silva, editor of the Indian publication *The Queer Chronicle*. "The venues for these lie scattered and are dependent on the venue owner's inclination towards being queer-friendly. There is no existence of a 'Gay Village' anywhere in India. Social networking sites like Facebook are our virtual gay village."

Though there is limited awareness in society, influences from Western cultures have impacted attitudes toward gay issues in India. As other countries expand gay rights and influential figures support such movements, these changes are being reflected in Indian culture.

"Recently the globalization of media has helped to raise issues related to sexuality," said Vidheesh, who is gay but is out to only a few select friends and family members in India. "Traditionally the Indian movies have **caricatured** the homosexuals as **effeminate** characters. However, some sincere attempts to seriously depict the context of sexuality have come of late."

Like many of his gay friends, Vidheesh is cautious about who knows about his sexual orientation. He fears his family could not understand and that they would blame themselves and be disappointed in him. While this attitude is not uncommon anywhere in the world, in India, it's especially significant because the culture revolves around the family.

D'Silva notes that the strength of the family's influence is enough to keep many people in the closet. "Family is very important to almost all Indians and running the risk of hurting them in any way is quite out of the question," he said. "The additional risks that [gay people] could face are being evicted from the family home and having all familial and financial ties cut off."

He explains that because the expectation of having a wife and children is so deeply engrained in every man's mind, many who know they are homosexual will still get married to please their family and

What's That Mean?

Caricatured means to depict a person in strongly stereotyped ways for comic reasons.

A man who is *effeminate* exhibits traditionally "feminine" behavior. The term is usually considered an insult.

society. This makes them susceptible to being black-mailed, which is a common way that gay people are harassed in India.

"So more often than not, gay men (and women) will fall in line with their family's expectations of getting married and starting a family," he said. "Most of these continue to lead a double life, in secrecy and in fear of being **outed** at some point of time."

In a culture where arranged marriages are still part of the tradition, Vidheesh knows of gay people who have been forced into marriage by their unsupportive families. He's also heard many stories of gay people being attacked by "hooligans who leverage on the very secret nature of sexual identity."

What's That Mean?

To be **outed** is to be publically exposed as a gay person, usually against your will.

But as laws continue to change, members of the Indian gay community are hopeful that public opinion on gay issues will also change. And that begins with awareness.

"By and large, the community is treated with derision and since the Delhi High Court ruling, with some amount of contempt as we are now more visible and this is something that society cannot come to terms with," said D'Silva. "As long as we were out of sight,

Henna designs like those shown here are traditionally female ornamentation in India, but this "hijra" activist had appropriated the cultural gender symbol. For Hindi speakers, the word "hijra" refers to transgenders and gays. Historically, hijras were once revered and respected in India, but when the British took over India, hijras became subject to movement restrictions, heightened surveillance, and warrant-less searches and seizures. In the twentieth century, most hijras could only find acceptance as performers, commercial sex workers, and panhandlers, but today, a pro-hijra movement has emerged, and hijras are working to regain the political power they once possessed.

EXTRA INFO

Arranged marriages are still common practice in many traditional families from India and other parts of Asia. In these cultures, couples do not get to know each other through dating; instead, parents search for compatible partners for their children. These families, including the young adults involved, view this as completely normal and acceptable. As the world becomes more Westernized, some young adults from these cultures are beginning to date, but they still tend to view arranged marriages as an option they can fall back on if they are unable or unwilling to spend the time and effort necessary to find spouses on their own.

we were out of mind. It is a pipe dream to wipe the slate clean, but gay activists and groups across the country are trying to help people understand us better and emphasize the need to have mutual respect and co-exist."

FIND OUT MORE ON THE INTERNET

Gay India and Indian Gay and Lesbian Resources
www.utopia-asia.com/tipsindi.htm

Gay South Africa
www.globalgayz.com/country/South % 20Africa/view/ZAF/gay-south-africa-the-new-scene-2

READ MORE ABOUT IT

Shahani, Parmesh. *Gay Bombay: Globalization, Love, and (Be)longing in Contemporary India*. New Delhi, India: SAGE Publications India, 2008.

Vasu, Reddy. *From Social Silence to Social Science: Same-Sex Sexuality, HIV & AIDS, and Gender in South Africa*. Pretoria, South Africa: Human Sciences Research Council, 2010

BIBLIOGRAPHY

Amnesty International. www.amnestyusa.org (5 May 2010).

Australian Marriage Equality. www.australianmarriageequality. com/civilunions.htm (5 May 2010).

Bennett, Rosemary. "Church 'Out of Touch' as Public Supports Equal Rights for Homosexuals." *The Times (UK),* June 27, 2009.

Equal Marriage for Same-Sex Couples. www.equalmarriage.ca (4 May 2010).

"Gay Couple Thrilled with an 'Amazing' Wedding." *CTV News,* June 1, 2005.

"Gay Marriage Around the Globe." *BBC,* December 22, 2005.

"Gay Marriage Law Comes into Effect in Mexico City." *BBC,* March 4, 2010.

"Gay Rights Around the World." *Newsweek,* February 22, 2010.

"Gay Rights Win in South Africa." *BBC,* October 9, 1998.

Gettleman, Jeffrey. "Americans' Role Seen in Uganda Anti-Gay Push." *The New York Times,* January 3, 2010.

Gomez, Edward M. "In the Caribbean, Anti-Gay Bigotry Thrives." *San Francisco Gate,* March 26, 2007.

Hines, Horace. "It Wasn't a Gay March!" *Jamaica Observer,* April 15, 2010.

Human Rights Campaign. www.hrc.org (6 May 2010).

Human Rights Watch. www.hrw.org (6 May 2010).

International Gay and Lesbian Human Rights Commission. www.iglhrc.org (6 May 2010).

Jones, Michael A. "A Few Statistics on LGBT Issues." *Change.org*, October 5, 2008.

Jones, Michael A. "Caribbean Attitudes Toward Homosexuality Changing, But Violence Toward LGBT People Remains Common." *Change.org*, October 13, 2008.

Martin, Michael. "U.S. Evangelical Leaders Blamed For Uganda Anti-Gay Sentiment." *National Public Radio,* December 18, 2009.

McLeod, Dwayne. "Gays Must Leave Today." *The Jamaica Star*, April 26, 2007.

Meldrum, Andrew. "Rainbow Planet: The Worldwide Struggle for Gay Rights." *GlobalPost,* February 3, 2010.

Nullis, Claire. "Same-Sex Law Takes Effect in South Africa." *Washington Post*, December 1, 2006.

Padgett, Tim. "The Most Homophobic Place on Earth?" *Time,* April 12, 2006.

Pleming, Sue. "In a Turnaround, U.S. Signs U.N. Gay Rights Document." *Reuters,* March 18, 2009.

Poddar, Mansi. "India Decriminalizes Gay Sex." *The Huffington Post,* July 2, 2009.

South Africa.info. www.southafrica.info (8 May 2010).

Staff. "South Africa to Have Gay Weddings." *BBC,* December 1, 2005.

Struck, Doug. "Same-Sex Marriage Advances in Canada." *The Washington Post*, June 29, 2005.

U.S. Department of State. www.state.gov (9 May 2010).

INDEX

ABOUT THE AUTHOR AND THE CONSULTANT

Jaime A. Seba's involvement in LGBT issues began in 2004, when she helped open the doors of the Pride Center of Western New York, which served a community of more than 100,000 people. As head of public education and outreach, she spearheaded one of the East Coast's first crystal methamphetamine awareness and harm reduction campaigns. She also wrote and developed successful grant programs through the Susan G. Komen Breast Cancer Foundation, securing funding for the region's first breast cancer prevention program designed specifically for gay, bisexual, and transgender women. Jaime studied political science at Syracuse University before switching her focus to communications with a journalism internship at the Press & Sun-Bulletin in Binghamton, New York, in 1999. She is currently a freelance writer based in Seattle.

James T. Sears specializes in research in lesbian, gay, bisexual, and transgender issues in education, curriculum studies, and queer history. His scholarship has appeared in a variety of peer-reviewed journals and he is the author or editor of twenty books and is the Editor of the *Journal of LGBT Youth*. Dr. Sears has taught curriculum, research, and LGBT-themed courses in the departments of education, sociology, women's studies, and the honors college at several universities, including: Trinity University, Indiana University, Harvard University, Penn State University, the College of Charleston, and the University of South Carolina. He has also been a Research Fellow at Center for Feminist Studies at the University of Southern California, a Fulbright Senior Research Southeast Asia Scholar on sexuality and culture, a Research Fellow at the University of Queensland, a consultant for the J. Paul Getty Center for Education and the Arts, and a Visiting Research Lecturer in Brazil. He lectures throughout the world.